THE HEART OF A PSALMIST

SPIRITUAL POETRY FOR THE HEART & SOUL

LADY STEPHANIE WYATT

VOL NO. 1

ACKNOWLEDGEMENTS

To my beautiful family and friends: thanks for believing in me! A very special thanks to Apostle JL Bryant, who spoke prophetically over me regarding this project. I appreciate you, man of God & my Zoom Family. To my Beautiful Mother, who's always there encouraging me to press towards the mark and reach my goal. I love you! To my 3 beautiful children: Gerae (Nakisha), Caprice and Victoria, thanks for believing in me. To my sister in Christ, Naurice Haynes, thanks for your undying support. This is one of many books you can carry throughout the generations. To Apostle Terry Cason Jr.: thank you for being a good friend and brother in the Lord, **Iron sharpens Iron!** Thank you, India Jenkins and Erica Suell: my two precious jewels. Thank you, Sparkle D. Smith, for your guidance, direction and insight in coaching me along this book completion process.

This has been an incredible journey. I cried many nights, wondering when, how and what my book would look like. I am walking in my purpose and fulfilling my greatest dream, which is fulfilling God's purpose. I appreciate my Lord and Saviour Jesus Christ for blessing me with the gift of writing prophetic poetry. I hope this book will be a blessing and an encouragement to those who are hurting and in need of spiritual healing. This book is designed for those in need of healing of the heart, mind, body, soul and spirit. Thanks to each and every one of you for believing in this dream. A special thanks to Pastor Vernon Norris and Lady Janice Norris and the Blessed Temple COGIC for your prayers and support. All pictures and photography produced by Lady/Prophetess Stephanie Wyatt.

I love the Lord, for he has dealt bountifully with me. Psalms 3:3.

Love Always,

Lady Stephanie Wyatt

INTRO

This book began over 20 years ago when I began to write some of the poems. I was inspired to write this book during the beginning of the pandemic. It was during that time, I was stricken with COVID-19, pneumonia and fell on my right hip. During my recovery process, I began to pull out all my poems and write new ones as the spirit led me. This book demonstrates the heart I have for God and his love for me. Now I really know the true meaning of being in the secret place, basking in his presence. We sometimes don't understand the why's of when we go through certain trials, tribulations and pain. It is during that valley period where he is birthing an anointing and purpose for your life greater than the intensity of the valley experience. As you seek him, you begin to understand the purpose of the valley/wilderness experience, as well as the tests, trials and tribulations.

As a result, I can truly say I have a heart of a psalmist.

Search me oh God and know my heart. Try me and know my thoughts. And see if there be any wicked way in me, lead me in the way everlasting. Psalm 139:23-24

As you read my book, it displays the love I have for Abba Father & his son Jesus Christ. Each poem was written under the direction of the Holy Spirit, of his healing power, love, mercy, shelter in the time of every storm, his faithfulness, and his spirit that never departs. This book is dedicated to my Grandmother, Irene Parker. I know she would be extremely proud of me. I'm missing you every day.

TABLE OF CONTENTS

POEM 1

THE PSALMIST'S HEART

***I love the Lord because he has heard my voice
and my supplications. Psalm 116:1***

I love the Lord with all my heart; he is so dear to me. I'll serve him all my days and live victoriously.

God delivered me from Satan's snare and the counsel of the wicked. He is almighty, divine, awesome, powerful and splendid.

He planted me by a living stream and listened to every prayer I sang; "YAHWEH" keep me near to thee for in you my righteousness is complete.

Your words to my heart are more soothing than oil. I'm purified in your holy soil. This sweet communion will never part. This is the sound of pure worship from a psalmist's heart.

POEM 2

FAITH

So then Faith cometh by hearing, and hearing from the word of God. Romans 10:17

Faith to speak life! Faith that gives sight! Faith to live abundantly! Faith to walk circumspectly.

Faith that mends broken hearts! Faith that won't ever depart! Faith that can't be stopped; Faith that can't be blocked.

Faith cannot be destroyed, depleted, mistreated, undermined or defeated. Faith to receive, achieve, that brings relief in the midst of strife & grief. Faith in lying down to sleep! Faith each day as I awake! Faith in every little step I take!

Faith that is not broken. Let's put our faith in motion without commotion, erosion, corrosion. Faith should be our daily devotion. Faith, Faith and more Faith are all we need; Faith the size of a mustard seed.

A Faith that's strong, powerful, undying and guaranteed.

POEM 3

SEEK ME

And those who seek me early and diligent will find me. Proverbs 8:17

Seek me, Seek me, seek my face. Daily dwell in that hidden place. I long to be in your presence where there's fullness and joy. As I seek you, I learn of your characteristics more, more, and more.

Seek and you will find those things that are concerning you. I've got in mind to prosper you, exalt you all in my own time. Stay humble, daily pursue me with all thy heart and might. Keep walking by faith and not by sight. Seek me in the morning, noon and night. I will guide you to the light.

Seek me and live, in my service diligently give. Don't seek after vainglory. Enter into God's presence and tell your story. I am omnipresent and know what you need; if only my face, you will seek, not the nouns, people, places or things. I am Jehovah, your God, and I will never change.

I have the best stimulus package you'll ever need; all I'm asking is ....that you only

SEEK ME.

POEM 4

WAIT ON YOU

They that wait upon the Lord shall renew their strength. Isaiah 40:31

I will wait patiently on thee, for you have heard my desperate cry; your feathers have wiped the tears from my eyes.

Day and night, my soul panteth for only you, your right hand, and holy arm has the power to pull me through. Each storm or hurricane that brings life's pain, my heart will take courage during the thunder and rain.

You will provide me shelter and cover me with your wings, and my heart will proclaim and sing, "YOU'RE THE SUN IN MY HORIZON," I can see you now arising.

As I wait on you, please grant me abundant grace; come fill me with your warm embrace, strengthen my steps to endure this race.

As I enter into your Holy of Holy Gates, where prayer & consecration is my fate, I will patiently WAIT ON YOU!

POEM 5

I WILL PRAISE YOU

I will bless the Lord at all times and his praise shall continually be in my mouth. Psalm 34:1

I will praise you thru my pain

I will praise you thru the rain

I will praise you in the valley low, on the mountain high. For you know what's best for me though my weary eyes can't see; you have the perfect plan for me.

With my lips; I will bless you thus, will I praise thee.

Jehovah Gmolah - my restorer

Jehovah Rapha- my healer

Jehovah Jireh- my provider

Jehovah Rohi- my shepherd who leads

Jehovah Gibbor- God almighty my soul worships thee.

From the depth of my heart, mind, body, and spirit;

Satan get behind me, you can't hinder. God is still Jehovah

El Elyon the sovereign one in control, for this is just a light affliction .... for God to display his power and his splendor.

Yes, you get the glory thru my pain.

Yes, you get the glory thru the rain.

You get the glory, thru all my tears.

You get the glory when things appear unclear.

My eyes are opened..... I now see your love, mercy, and grace... your perfect plan it's in its rightful place. It's working for my good, and the perfection of my soul...... I've been thru the fire, I'm coming forth as pure GOLD.

POEM 6

ᏑGOT YOU

Casting all your care upon him; for He careth for you. I Peter 5:7

I heard the voice of Jesus saying, come unto me and rest. I'm your heavenly father, so I know what's best. I am the creator from the beginning to the end. Come sup and dwell with me, I'll abide within.

I won't ever leave you during this pandemic of perilous times. It's only to draw you closer so that I can call you mine. Draw nigh unto me, and I'll draw nigh unto you. I'll uphold you, keep you, uplift you, fill you, comfort and love you through and through.

Just like I led Moses and the children of Israel across the Red Sea, I am Jehovah Shammah that carries you to your destiny.

Stand strong! See my salvation. Don't fret! My love is always here. I've never left. The essence of what God's heart is saying; He has us in his care each and every day.

Hold on to my promises; I will never fail. I took on your healing with 1 hammer and 3 nails. Bow down and worship my name, my word, the Best-selling book ''Goes in Heaven's Hall of Fame.

When you are feeling lonely, afraid, depressed, rejected and confused; Just remember my children....... I GOT YOU!

POEM 7

I WILL SING

I will sing unto the Lord as long as I live. Psalm 104:33

I will sing of your goodness and sing of your grace; no other person can ever take your place. I will sing a song of Victory, never forgetting the day you'd set me free.

I will sing of your protection and how you kept me safe; I will sing a song, what it means to seek your face. I will sing of your healing power and sing of your sovereignty.

I will sing to you my Lord, my Saviour; my soon coming king. I will sing of your faithfulness and mercies untold. I will sing of heavens streets paved in gold.

I will sing and lift my eyes unto the hills, knowing that you will fight my battles only when I'm still. I will sing a song angels can't sing.

I'm singing, "'HOLY, HOLY, HOLY!" I've been redeemed by your name. I will sing of your handwork; you caused the sun to shine.

I will sing of having your sameness of mind. I will sing of your awesomeness towards the children of men. I will sing of your presence moving throughout the land.

I will sing, forever sing, my Saviour reigns, let heaven and earth decree..... A new song I will sing.

POEM 8

SAVE ME, LORD !

Heal me oh Lord and I will be healed. Save me oh Lord and I will be saved. For thou art my praise. Jeremiah 17:14

Don't allow my soul to be overtaken by a Spiritual Pandemic. Don't let my stagnation become a hindrance. Save me from me, myself and I. Save me from all selfishness and contagious pride.

Each day, help me with my Spiritual Protection Equipment (SPE) so I won't be infected with those spiritually transmitted diseases. (STD's) Help those who have refused to change their ways, believing that X,Y and Z is the way to stay.

Save me, so I won't become a potential adverse event, a biohazard, infectious waste and spreading vicious intent. Save me from the viruses of doubt. Save me from those spiritual root canals that seep... rotten out of my mouth.

You know when I'm right and when I'm wrong; search

my heart all day long. Expose anything that should not be, remove it "LORD SAVE ME." Let me be spiritually fit, effective, not consumed with sin that causes spirit quarantine.

Lord, let me be a beneficial bill of health washed and clean. Strengthen me to promote spiritual decontamination in a relevant way... SAVE ME! SAVE ME, LORD... This is my prayer today!

POEM 9

ARE YOU SEEKING THE KINGDOM OR A THINGDOM?

But seek ye first the kingdom of God and all his righteousness.... Matthew 6:33

The Bible tells us to seek ye first the Kingdom of God and all these things will be added unto you. We say, Yes Lord, your face I will seek.

Instead, we have other life obligations to meet: no prayer or fasting, not a single trace. We don't read our Bible as we run this race.

Chasing after righteousness is the only way to go. Instead, we chase after those things which cause us to lose our souls.

We seek people, places, and things to exalt ourselves with wealth and fame. We seek diamonds, rubies, riches of gold, but forgetting about heaven and the half untold.

God says: seek my face and not my hand; be bold, be courageous and walk as I command. With humble hearts, turn from your wicked ways, honor and live in my presence day by day.

Crave for my spirit and kingdom thinking, come judgement day; it will be a rude awakening.

Take no thought of what you should eat or drink. I am Jehovah "the Great," and won't leave you in a desolate, dry place.

Be ye cleansed through my word which brings you life; be ye delivered from all pain, envy, evil, malice, hatred, uncleanness and strife; serve me with all your heart, mind, strength and might.

This question, I propose to the believers today: Are you seeking my kingdom or a thingdom/ or just living in any kind of way?

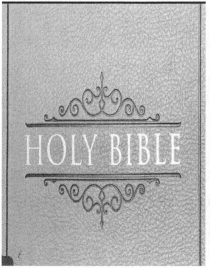

POEM 10

YOU ARE MY STRENGTH

But I will sing of your strength........Psalm 28:7

You are my strength when I weep. You are my strength when I can't sleep. You are my strength when I get weak. You are my strength when I can't see. You are my strength when I can't speak. YOUR STRENGTH IS STRONGER THAN A LION'S DARK MANE. IT SOOTHES MY FEARS & TAKES AWAY MY PAIN. YOU ARE MY STRENGTH, IN EVERY STEP I TAKE AS MY FEET ARE PLANTED--- WITH PURPOSE ORDAINED. YOU STRENGTHEN MY MIND, BODY, HEART, SOUL AND SPIRIT; I'LL SERVE YOU FOR THE REST OF MY LIFE UNRESTRAINED. YOU ARE MY STRENGTH & THE LIGHT OF MY SALVATION; YOUR JOY IS MY STRENGTH IN TROUBLED TIMES AND TRIBULATIONS. YOUR STRENGTH GIVES ME LOVE & CONSOLATIONS. I LOOK TO YOU WHEN MY STRENGTH IS GONE. YOU ARE THE LIFTER OF MY HEAD, SO I CAN JOURNEY ON. YOUR BLOOD GIVES ME STRENGTH FROM DAY TO DAY. YOUR STRENGTH NEVER LEAVES ME CONFUSED, SORROWFUL, HEARTBROKEN OR

DISMAYED. YOU ARE MY STRENGTH LIKE NONE OTHER THAT STICKS CLOSER THAN ANY BROTHER. YOUR STRENGTH IS ALL THAT I NEED. YOUR STRENGTH KEEPS ME GROUNDED, COVERED, SECURE, ANCHORED & COMPLETE. THANK YOU, LORD; YOU ARE MY STRENGTH!

POEM 11

YOUR WILL

Thy kingdom come thy will be done..... Matthew 6:9

I relinquish my will and my ways; for you Lord I will obey. I give you my body as a living sacrifice, serve you with all my heart, soul, strength and might.

For you know the plans you have for me; if I yield to your will constantly, dying daily to self, flesh, my strong volition, dying to the cares of this world and all its fictions.

Seeking and thirsting for your will to be complete, my soul cries YES! YES! YES! I'll give you all of me.

Withholding nothing! Not one ounce or drop, chasing after your righteousness as I've always been taught.

I will sing and walk in my gift prophetically, seeking after you my savior and my divine king.

As I lay me down to sleep each night, my heart cries, " Let your will be done; I relinquish mine.

POEM 12

GOD'S LOVE

For God so loved the world that he gave his only begotten son that whosoever believeth in him shall not perish but have everlasting life. John 3:16

I was sinking deep in sin. God's love lifted me. His power gave me life and life abundantly. God's love helped me when I was down. His love never makes me frown.

His love heals us from every diabolic memory. It surrounds us like the roaring sea. It smothers me like the waves and makes me complete, my life in sync to God's heartbeat.

God's love has dealt bountifully with me. This is the happiest place I could ever be. Wrapped in his love both day and night, I will never have to walk in fright.

God's love keeps me safe. It covers me from that ungodly place. God's love is like a hammer that breaks a rock in twain. His love covers a multitude of shame.

God's love will never embarrass you. It's like a beautiful

tune that won't leave you gloom. God's love is a melody that only my heart can sing, "Saviour" to the cross I cling.

God's love is the greatest romance we could ever seek, falling down and worshiping at his feet. God's greatest gift was Jesus, his only son..... he gave him to us as the begotten one.

Remember..... God's love is the lifter of my soul. His love is pure, honest and brings joy and truth. GOD IS LOVE... AND HE LOVES ME, AND GOD LOVES YOU!

POEM 13

THRONE ROOM WORSHIP

After this I beheld and lo a great multitude of all nations and kindred and tongues, and stood before the throne of the Lamb of God. Revelation 7:9

Last night, I was awakened by an angel of light. He said, Come with me to this special place. When we arrived, I saw and heard psalms, hymns, harps, strings and beautiful melodies.

God's anointing power showered down on me. Songs of "How Great Thou Art " my Saviour God to thee.

You are Alpha and Omega. You deserve my praise, a sweet aroma of righteousness in purity he reigns.

I'm engulfed in his presence. The glory is so bright, chairs of pearls, walls of Jasper and robes of snow-white.

I bring you all of me as I lay before his throne, surrendering to my king alone.

The sweet sound of worship, so soothing to my ears, my soul is joyously overwhelmed by what my heart feels.

I can barely stand. I'm bowing at his feet, just seeing the holy fire. All I can do is weep.

Hallelujah! Hallelujah! The host of Seraphim sang, " For thou art worthy" ... the Lamb of God that was slain.

I'd placed you here to be alone with me.... Better is one day in your court; than one thousand elsewhere; I'd rather be. There is nothing like a one on one throne room experience with thee.

POEM 14

THE LIVING LAMB

Worthy is the Lamb that was slain to receive power and wisdom and riches and strength and honor and glory. Revelation 5:12

Mary had a little lamb and Jesus is his name. For God so loved the world that he gave his only begotten son that whosoever believes in him should not perish but have everlasting life.

I am the Way, the Truth and the Light. I will be your comforter, morning, noon and night. Jesus, Jesus, yes, that's who I am. I hold the power of the world in my hands!

I am Alpha and Omega from the beginning to the end. I am the King of kings, I am the Lord of lords, I am the prince of peace, the balm of Gilead who heals you from your sinful disease.

Jesus! Jesus! Yes that's who I am! I hold the power of the world in my hands. I died on the cross so that you would not be lost.

Demons tremble at the sound of my name. I can heal the sick, raise the dead and take away your shame. Jesus! Jesus!

Yes, that's who I am, for I have the proof of the nail scars in my hand. I can calm the storm in every raging sea and cause you to walk on waters peacefully.

Jesus! Jesus! Yes, that's who I am. For I am the son of the GREAT I AM!

So just in case you forgot who I am, I am Jesus, Jesus, Jesus, Jesus, Christ. I am the living Lamb.

POEM 15

GOD'S SPIRIT

Not by might, not by power but by my spirit says the Lord. Zechariah 4:6

God's spirit will never leave you, destroy or abuse. His spirit won't leave you broken or misused. God's spirit will be your guide and not leave your side.

God's spirit is truth. It doesn't make you anxious or confused. God's spirit is uplifting and kind. It will give you peace sublime. God's spirit is life.

It will keep us from all envy, evil and strife. God's spirit whispers gently in our ears, "saying," hold to your confession and just be still.

God's spirit is the calmness in the midst of life's storms. His spirit saves, delivers, and transforms.

God's spirit is everlasting and his testimony is pure. His spirit is faithful, loving and His mercies always endure.

God's spirit causes the believers to win. The question I'm asking: Do you have God's spirit outwardly and in?

POEM 16

VICTORIOUS LIVING

***Now thanks to God who causes us to triumph in Christ, and makes us manifest the fragrance of his knowledge by us in every place.* II Corinthians 2:14**

Victory is mine as I daily declare. My life has been changed by his word, healed by his divine power, I decree victory sublime.

I will sing praises, songs, testimonies of how God is moving; every day, through his righteousness, I am renewing.

I declare of his goodness and miraculous blessings as he performs. I give thanks for coming through every mountain and every storm.

To seek and save those who are lost, encouraging our brothers and sisters at any cost. I enter into his presence, so my healing can begin. My daily prayer is LORD deliver me from the cycle of sin.

Keep me from the snare of Satan's deadly device; make me a sanctuary to shine bright.

I am a beacon of light, serving him with thanksgiving. No longer a defeated life-- I now walk, talk, live, eat, breathe and sleep FOR VICTORIOUS LIVING.

POEM 17

GIVE THANKS

Oh give thanks to the Lord. Oh give thanks in everything, for this is the will of Christ Jesus concerning you. I Thessalonians 5:18

Give thanks to God in all things; serve him with a grateful heart. Don't let his praises from your mouth ever depart.

Give thanks during seasons of doubt. I give thanks because you will bring me out! Give thanks for the birds that sing. Give thanks to him day by day.

Give thanks when we kneel & pray. I know he is listening to every word I say. Give thanks for blessings one by one! Give thanks for Jesus, God's begotten son!

Give thanks for his healing power that cures. Give thanks for his blood that washes us pure. Give thanks for the food you eat. Give thanks before you lay down to sleep.

Giving thanks for God is so good. Give thanks while sometimes being misunderstood. In your word, it says to Give Thanks for this is your will concerning me.

Therefore, I will thank you throughout eternity. You gave me life and life more abundantly. I'm thankful, alive and living triumphantly.

My soul sings.. "Oh give thanks unto thee."

POEM 18

STAND

Stand fast therefore in the liberty wherewith Christ has made us free. Galatians 5:1

I stand in your power, love, mercy and grace. I stand steadfast in this daily race. I stand in, knowing you will give me the victory. You are the greatest vindicator indeed.

I stand on your word for daily guidance that adds no sorrow, trusting only in you for a better tomorrow.

I stand when things turn UPSIDE DOWN, conquering the battle to receive my crown. I stand in the midst my fears, thanking you, father, for wiping my tears.

I stand in the majesty of your faithfulness; I'm covered in favor and clothed in righteousness. I stand in all ABBA has promised me; it's not I but the Christ that's within thee.

I stand against Satan and all of his demonic antics; the spirit of God will demolish his tactics. I stand in faith without wrath or doubt. I have true confidence that you will bring me out.

I stand with my face turned towards the wall; your mighty hand won't let me fall. I stand, therefore, in the liberty where Christ has set me free and stand strong through tumultuous adversities.

On Christ the solid rock I stand, all other ground is sinking sand. Therefore my brethren put on the whole armor; that ye may be able to stand.

Having done all to STAND, JUST STAND!

POEM 19

LORD, FORGIVE ME

Create in me a clean heart, and renew a right spirit in me. Psalm 51:10

The meaning of forgiveness is defined as a conscious, deliberate decision to release feelings of treatment or vengeance towards individuals who have harmed you.

Forgive me, Lord, for the cancerous grudges I've held in my heart.

When I stand before you, I don't want you to SAY DEPART.

Forgive me, Lord, when I failed to put on the shield of faith, for it's impossible to please you when I'm spiritually displaced. Forgive me, Lord, for the times I neglected to read your word for guidance. I was being rebellious and defiant.

Forgive me, Lord, for not putting on the breastplate of righteousness. I've allowed my life to become a complete mess. I did not honor you in prayer and spiritual consecration. I blamed others for my demise and spreading malicious gossip and lies.

Forgive me, Lord, for not loving my parents as I should. I was angry and walked away like a wayward thug hood. Forgive me, Lord, for slandering those I love, judging others' shortcomings as I stayed a wretch undone. Forgive me, Lord, for the secret sins that caused pain and embarrassment in my life. My generational seeds have been paying that price.

Forgive me, Lord, for the times I overlooked when I saw a person that had nothing to eat. Forgive me, Lord, for not thanking you before lying down to sleep.

Forgive me, Lord, for the time I was not understanding of my children. Instead, I tore them down with my harsh and shrewd opinions. Forgive me, Lord, for those I've hurt with my anger, wrath, and hatred ways, saying, "I hope they get theirs soon someday."

Asking for forgiveness is not for others but for me! Especially when I pray, LORD MAKE ME MORE LIKE THEE. How can I be like you when carrying this unforgiveness around? For this has kept my soul enslaved with wounds rooted and bound.

Father, on this day, create in me a clean heart. Pluck me, prune me, strip me from all bitterness, and selfish pride. I surrender to your will to be set free. It's plain to see, God. Woe is me !!!

I'm faulty, filthy, hostile, cruel, disobedient, unforgiving, untrue, and unclean. I take the blame. Father, please FORGIVE ME.

POEM 20

I CAN'T BREATHE

The Spirit of God has made me and the breath of the Almighty gives me life. Job 33:4

Walking through life aimlessly, without God's presence, I can't breathe. Singing a song without a tune make makes my world dark & gloom; eating food without a taste, your love can never be replaced.

Each day as I seek your face, I'm in that Godly place. Each breath I take, you fill my lungs. I will praise you with ten thousand tongues.

You are the King that is soon to come. Each day of my life, I'll endlessly sing; I need thee, oh, I need thee.

Your faithfulness is greater than the ocean of a raging sea. Without your breath, my life would be empty.

Like a ship that drifts with no gale, a sinking ship without a sail, your mercy will never fail. Your breath is the center of my being; in you, Lord, I lift my hands and sing. Without you, Lord, I CAN'T BREATHE.

POEM 21

YOU BELONG TO ME

But you are a chosen people, a royal priesthood, a holy nation in God's own possession I Peter 2:9

FATHER SAYS; YOU BELONG TO ME AND NO ONE ELSE. IN ME, THERE IS SHELTER, REFUGE, HEALTH AND WEALTH. LOOK UNTO MY HILLS FROM WITH COMETH YOUR HELP.

FROM THE BEGINNING OF THE WORLD, I CALLED YOUR NAME. I MADE YOU AFTER MY LIKENESS AND IMAGE, SO I STAKE MY CLAIM. I PLACED THE SEAL OF HEAVEN UPON YOUR SOUL WITH THE ANOINTING OF MY FIERY FLAME.

I PLACED YOUR HEARTBEAT IN SYNC WITH MINE, SO I COULD HEAR YOUR EVERY CRY. I ESTABLISHED YOUR STEPS, YOUR EVERY BEING .... I CREATED YOU TO LIVE, WALK, GIVE, SURRENDER AND WORSHIP ME.

YOU DID NOT CHOOSE ME, I CHOSE YOU. I GAVE YOU A JOB THAT YOU MUST DO. TELL THE WORLD THAT I

AM ALIVE, TELL THEM HOW I SET YOU ASIDE. REACH THE LOST WITH MY LOVE; TELL THEM THEY ARE THE APPLE OF MY EYE, FOR THEM MY SON "'JESUS" DIED. USE YOUR MOUTHPIECE AS AN INSTRUMENT OF LIGHT --- LET IT SHINE THROUGH THE WORLD ALL DAY, ALL NIGHT.

PRESENT TO ME EACH DAY AS A LIVING SACRIFICE, BE HOLY, AND ACCEPTABLE ONLY IN MY SIGHT. TELL ME, YOU WILL SERVE ME WITH ALL OF YOUR STRENGTH AND MIGHT. I CARE ABOUT EVERYTHING CONCERNING YOU; JUST REMEMBER MY PROMISES WILL ALWAYS REMAIN TRUE. I AM CONSTANTLY GROOMING, SHAPING, PRUNING, PREPARING A PLACE FOR YOU TO MEET WITH ME.... OH YES! THAT PLACE IS THE SACRED GETHASMENE WHERE YOU WILL CRY BLOOD, SWEAT, AND TEARS AND SAY ---- YES !!!! TO MY ULTIMATE WILL. THIS IS THE GREATEST LOVE AFFAIR OF ALL TIMES, WHERE YOU CALL ME YOURS AND I CALL YOU MINE. YOU'RE MY BEST MASTERPIECE, CAN'T YOU SEE? IT'S OBVIOUS STEPHANIE YOU BELONG TO ME.

Made in the USA
Las Vegas, NV
08 March 2022